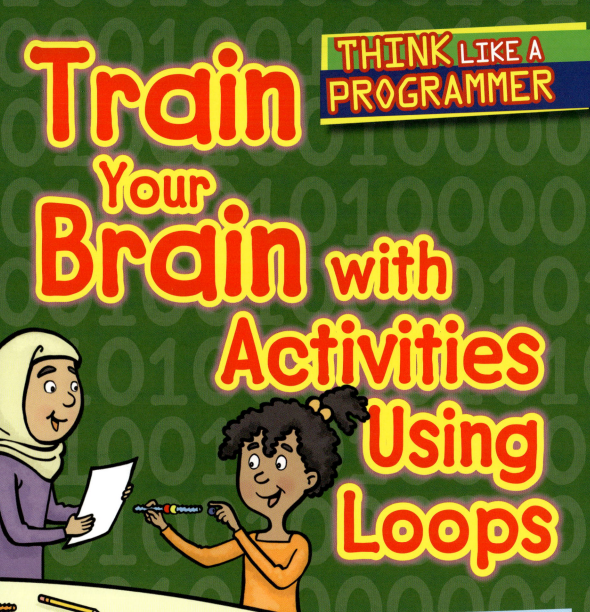

Train Your Brain with Activities Using Loops

THINK LIKE A PROGRAMMER

by Emilee Hillman

illustrated by Dana Regan

Published in 2020 by Cavendish Square Publishing, LLC
243 5th Avenue, Suite 136, New York, NY 10016

Copyright © 2020 by Cavendish Square Publishing, LLC

First Edition

No part of this publication may be reproduced, stored in a retrieval system, or transmitted in any form or by any means—electronic, mechanical, photocopying, recording, or otherwise—without the prior permission of the copyright owner. Request for permission should be addressed to Permissions, Cavendish Square Publishing, 243 5th Avenue, Suite 136, New York, NY 10016. Tel (877) 980-4450; fax (877) 980-4454.

Website: cavendishsq.com

This publication represents the opinions and views of the author based on his or her personal experience, knowledge, and research. The information in this book serves as a general guide only. The author and publisher have used their best efforts in preparing this book and disclaim liability rising directly or indirectly from the use and application of this book.

All websites were available and accurate when this book was sent to press.

Library of Congress Cataloging-in-Publication Data

Names: Hillman, Emilee, author. | Regan, Dana, illustrator.
Title: Train your brain with activities using loops / Emilee Hillman ; illustrator, Dana Regan.
Description: New York : Cavendish Square, [2019] | Series: Think like a programmer | Includes bibliographical references and index. | Audience: Grades 2-5
Identifiers: LCCN 2018059114 (print) | LCCN 2019000358 (ebook) | ISBN 9781502648174 (ebook) | ISBN 9781502648167 (library bound) | ISBN 9781502648143 (pbk.) | ISBN 9781502648150 (6 pack)
Subjects: LCSH: Computer programming--Juvenile literature. | Problem solving--Programming--Juvenile literature.
Classification: LCC QA76.52 (ebook) | LCC QA76.52 .H54 2019 (print) | DDC 005.1--dc23
LC record available at https://lccn.loc.gov/2018059114

Editorial Director: David McNamara
Editor: Kristen Susienka
Copy Editor: Nathan Heidelberger
Associate Art Director: Alan Sliwinski
Designer: Joe Parenteau
Illustrator: Dana Regan
Production Coordinator: Karol Szymczuk

Printed in the United States of America

Contents

INTRODUCTION ... 4
LOOP IT ... 6
BEAD PATTERNING ... 8
PATTERN PRECISION ... 10
THE SHAPE OF A LOOP ... 12
FIXING THE LOOP ... 14
LINE DANCE LOOP ... 16
BUILDING WITH SHAPES ... 18
NEW NOTEBOOK ... 20
A NEW STORY ... 22
PATCHWORK PERSONALITY ... 24
ART AND WORDS ... 26
TRASH TO TREASURE ... 28
GLOSSARY ... 30
FIND OUT MORE ... 31
INDEX ... 32

Introduction

Computer programmers are great thinkers. They use their minds to invent cool games and fun activities on a computer. If you want to be a computer programmer too, that's great! These activities will help you perfect your skills at identifying **patterns**. The best programmers understand how to organize a problem and make the steps easy to follow. Sometimes they do this by using patterns called **loops**. Loops repeat patterns for a certain number of times in a computer program.

This is all part of **computational thinking**. Despite the name, this way of thinking doesn't need a computer! All you have to do is think about how to solve problems, one step at a time.

These fun activities will help you train your brain to recognize information and patterns. You'll also learn that sometimes patterns aren't easy to find. That is why it's important to understand and practice computational thinking. This is how you learn to think like a programmer!

Loop It

NUMBER OF PLAYERS 1

TIME NEEDED
15–20 minutes

You'll Need
- Pencil
- Paper

ACTIVITY OVERVIEW

Programmers try to make **codes** run as easily as possible. That often means they find ways to simplify the code. One way to do this is by using loops. A loop is a way of simplifying a repeated activity in coding. Loops save time and energy! In this activity, you will think of a way to shorten a repeating song.

INSTRUCTIONS

To start, think of a simple song that repeats a lot. A few ideas are "The Ants Go Marching," "Old MacDonald," or "Wheels on the Bus."

Then, write down some motions for the parts of the song that repeat. After you have written down these motions, act out your song! The repeating motions in the song are the loop you just described.

Bead Patterning

NUMBER OF PLAYERS 2

TIME NEEDED

15–20 minutes

You'll Need
- Pencil
- Paper
- Colored beads
- Pipe cleaner

ACTIVITY OVERVIEW

Being able to identify and define patterns is a key skill in computer programming. Computational thinking involves recognizing when a pattern appears and using that pattern to help solve a tough problem. In this activity, you will make a pattern and then have a friend or family member repeat it.

INSTRUCTIONS

First, ask your parents to buy small colored beads and a pipe cleaner. Once you have those items, make a pattern with the beads by threading them onto the pipe cleaner. The pattern should repeat. Then, write directions for how to make your pattern and how many times it should repeat. After, give the directions to a friend or one of your family members. Were they able to follow the instructions to make the pattern?

Pattern Precision

NUMBER OF PLAYERS 1

TIME NEEDED

15–20 minutes

You'll Need
- Pencil
- Paper

ACTIVITY OVERVIEW

Turning simple repeated actions into loops is an important part of programming and computational thinking. However, it can often be difficult to decide how long or complex a loop should be. Even experienced **coders** struggle with this. In this activity, you will find a good way to identify a loop.

INSTRUCTIONS

Copy the letters below onto your piece of paper.

TADZRTADZRTADZRTADZRTADZR

Can you find a pattern in the letters? If so, how many times does it repeat? How could you describe the line to a friend? Write out a list of instructions to explain the pattern.

THINK ABOUT IT!

What if a few letters were missing from the line? How would you figure out what the pattern was then? Try it out with your friend, taking turns to invent new patterns.

The Shape of a Loop

NUMBER OF PLAYERS

TIME NEEDED

15–20 minutes

You'll Need
- Pencil
- Paper

ACTIVITY OVERVIEW

Loops are everywhere. In the real world, they happen every day. Sometimes loops are in code, a breakfast routine, or someone's sleeping habits. Recognizing and defining patterns is easy for a strong computational thinker because they realize how often these patterns appear in everyday life. In this activity, you will try to find a loop in shapes.

INSTRUCTIONS

First, study this pattern:

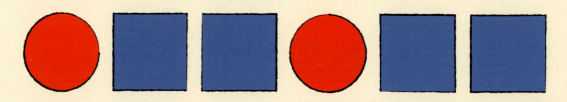

Then, write down what the pattern is. How many times does the pattern repeat? What shapes would come next if it continued? After you've answered the questions, see if you can write the pattern in a more simple way.

Fixing the Loop

NUMBER OF PLAYERS 2

TIME NEEDED
10–15 minutes

You'll Need
- Pencil
- Paper

ACTIVITY OVERVIEW

If something goes wrong in a computer **model**, the programmer has to check their work to find the problem. Often, that means finding the part of a pattern that is out of order and fixing it to match the rest of the pattern. In this activity, you will find mistakes in a pattern and fix them.

INSTRUCTIONS

Have a friend or family member think up a pattern of shapes and drawings. Then, have them draw it on a piece of paper for you. The pattern should have some mistakes, though! Can you spot the errors and fix the pattern? Next, switch places and see if your friend or family member can fix mistakes in something you draw.

THINK ABOUT IT!

Sometimes a line of code is so tough to follow that a programmer has to make a new pattern. What would happen if you drew totally random shapes and drawings? Can you and your friend or family member find a way to add and remove pieces to make a pattern?

Line Dance Loop

NUMBER OF PLAYERS

TIME NEEDED

15–20 minutes

You'll Need
- Pencil
- Paper

ACTIVITY OVERVIEW

Many computer programs follow patterns. Computer programmers need to be able to write patterns and make them repeat in a program. The more a program repeats, the easier it is to write the program's code. Many times, programmers need to write their code so that another programmer could understand and follow it if they took over the programming. In this activity, you will practice patterns in a dance and describe them to a friend.

INSTRUCTIONS

First, think about a simple dance you know well. Maybe "The Hokey Pokey" or "Head, Shoulders, Knees, and Toes." Next, practice the song so you know the steps. After you've mastered the moves, think about the dance steps. Do you notice that the steps repeat? Now, write out the basic steps of the dance. Then, find a way of arranging these simple steps. Your directions should include words like "repeat four times." This helps other people follow the dance with as few instructions as possible. Once you write the steps, try to follow them! Can you recreate the dance?

THINK ABOUT IT!

Sometimes, programmers use loops that change over time. A pattern might repeat, but a part of that pattern might be different with each repetition. The thing that changes is called a variable. For example, "The Hokey Pokey" uses a pattern of moves: put something in, put something out, put something in, shake it. But each time the pattern repeats, the body part doing the action changes: right hand, left hand, right foot, left foot. In this case, the body part is the variable.

Building with Shapes

NUMBER OF PLAYERS

TIME NEEDED

15–20 minutes

> **You'll Need**
> - Drawing supplies
> - Construction paper
> - Scissors

ACTIVITY OVERVIEW

Sharing and reusing information is important in computational thinking. Programmers share and reuse knowledge and resources all the time. By sharing, programmers can make their codes better. Coders also often have to take items or ideas already made and make them work for their project! In this activity, you will change shapes into fun objects.

INSTRUCTIONS

Using construction paper and scissors, cut out different shapes. Ideas are triangles, circles, and squares. Then, turn your shapes into things from real life! For example, a circle could become a wheel, a rectangle could become a truck, and a triangle could become a slice of pizza. How many different ways can you use the shapes to make something new? When you're finished, do the same activity but use two shapes together, like a triangle and a square. How many ideas can you come up with when you use two shapes together?

New Notebook

NUMBER OF PLAYERS

TIME NEEDED

20–30 minutes

You'll Need
- Paper
- Construction paper
- Scissors
- Stapler

ACTIVITY OVERVIEW

Often, computer programmers use code from other programmers. Programmers share information because good code can be used in many places. A programmer might change the code to fit their program. However, even when the code is very different between programs, a computational thinker can recognize the ways it has been altered and repurposed. In this activity, you will make an everyday object using simple items!

INSTRUCTIONS

To begin, start with a piece of construction paper. Fold the paper horizontally. Then, take some blank

pieces of white paper. Cut the white paper to match the height of the construction paper, or cut the construction paper to fit around the pages, depending on which is taller. Next, slip the blank pages inside the construction paper cover. Finally, staple the edges of the construction paper so it holds the pages together. By using two different kinds of paper, you have made your own notebook! Now, really make it your own by decorating it however you want.

A New Story

NUMBER OF PLAYERS

TIME NEEDED

20–30 minutes

ACTIVITY OVERVIEW

Parts of code are often shared between programmers. But programmers always change the code every time it is used. Sometimes, it's hard to tell it's the same code! Coders are good at finding new ways to use already existing code to help their projects. In this activity, you will exercise your imagination and computational thinking skills.

INSTRUCTIONS

To begin, ask your parents for some old magazines or newspapers. Then, cut out a picture from one

You'll Need
- Pencil
- Paper
- Scissors
- Glue
- Old magazines or newspapers

and glue it to a new piece of paper. Next, use the picture as inspiration. Write the first two sentences of a new story you think could match the picture.

Patchwork Personality

NUMBER OF PLAYERS

TIME NEEDED

15–20 minutes

ACTIVITY OVERVIEW

Computational thinking sometimes has you think through a problem using information from other problems. For example, sometimes coders use code from other coders to make their programs work. They change this code to fit their program. In this activity, you will use materials from other places to put together a **collage**. A collage is a mix of different photos to make one work of art.

You'll Need
- Paper
- Scissors
- Old magazines or newspapers
- Glue

INSTRUCTIONS

Start with some old magazines or newspapers. Next, cut out some pictures and words from them.

These pictures and words should describe you, your favorite things, and things you want to do when you grow up. Next, glue the pieces you've cut out onto a new piece of paper. This is how you make a collage. When you are done, write a few sentences about how using these old materials in a new way helped you create a collage about yourself.

Art and Words

NUMBER OF PLAYERS

TIME NEEDED

20–30 minutes

ACTIVITY OVERVIEW

Coders need code to make a program work. Lines of code can come from different places. Many coders use code from other programmers. Code from other programmers helps programmers complete other projects. Sometimes, the coders change the code to make their program better. In this activity, you will create a piece of art using other art.

INSTRUCTIONS

To start, use old magazines or newspapers to create a new piece of art. You can do this by cutting out parts of the newspapers or magazines. You can

You'll Need
- Scissors
- Glue
- Old magazines or newspapers
- Paper

cut them into small pieces or different shapes. You could take the eyes of one picture and put them on the face of another, for example. Glue the pictures to a blank piece of paper. This is a good way to understand how to take old material and make it into something new.

Trash to Treasure

NUMBER OF PLAYERS

TIME NEEDED

15–20 minutes

ACTIVITY OVERVIEW

Computer programmers know how to use other code and change it into new code. The new code works for their program. In this activity, you will take recycled items and turn them into a new item.

You'll Need
- Pencil
- Drawing supplies
- Paper
- Recyclable materials (cardboard, cans, etc.)

INSTRUCTIONS

First, get some items from your recycling bin and clean them. You will use these items later. Now, think of a new invention you can build with the items you chose. The invention could be a toy or a game. Next, draw a design for your invention. After that, write a list of the materials you will need. Once you have a design, try to build your invention. Did it come together the way you thought it would? What troubles did you face? How could you make the design better?

Glossary

CODE Instructions that a computer follows to work.

CODERS Another word for computer programmers.

COLLAGE Artwork made from other artwork or words, like magazine and newspaper photos or words.

COMPUTATIONAL THINKING A way of thinking where you break a big task into smaller tasks.

LOOPS Patterns that repeat many times.

MODEL A smaller version of a project.

PATTERNS Shapes, words, or numbers that repeat.

Find Out More

BOOKS

Cleary, Brian P. *Nothing Loopy About This: What Are Loops and Conditionals?* Coding is CATegorical. Minneapolis, MN: Millbrook Press, 2019.

Wainewright, Max. *How to Code: A Step-by-Step Guide to Computer Coding*. New York: Sterling Children's Publishing, 2016.

WEBSITE

Tynker: Coding for Kids

https://www.tynker.com

This website offers kids the opportunity to explore games and other activities that teach coding skills.

VIDEO

Kodable: Loops

https://www.youtube.com/watch?v=eSWCgZBSx_U&t

In this video, a computer science teacher explains, in simple terms, what loops are and how they work in computer programming.

Index

Entries in **boldface** are glossary terms.

code, 6, 12, 15, 16, 18, 20, 22, 24, 26, 28
coders (programmers), 4–5, 6, 10, 14–15, 16–17, 18, 20, 22, 24, 26, 28
collage, 24–25, 26–27
computational thinking, 5, 8, 10, 12, 18, 20, 22, 24
directions, 8–9, 11, 17
group activities, 8–9, 14–15
individual activities, 6–7, 10–11, 12–13, 16–17, 18–19, 20–21, 22–23, 24–25, 26–27, 28–29
loops, 4, 6–7, 10, 12, 17
mistakes, 14–15
model, 14
patterns, 4–5, 8–9, 10–11, 12–13, 14–15, 16–17
planning, 28–29
problem-solving, 4–5, 8, 24
reusing, 18–19, 20–21, 22–23, 24–25, 26–27, 28–29
sharing, 18, 20, 22
simplifying, 6, 13, 16–17
variable, 17